CHRISTINE TANZ

An Egg Is to Sit On

pictures by ROSEKRANS HOFFMAN

Lothrop, Lee & Shepard Company
A Division of William Morrow & Company, Inc.
New York

Library of Congress Cataloging in Publication Data

Tanz, Christine.
   An egg is to sit on.
   Summary: Children imitate such animal behavior as sitting on eggs, pocketing one's young, and making music with one's legs.
   I. Hoffman, Rosekrans.   II. Title.
PZ7.T1634Eg [E] 77-90534
ISBN 0-688-41811-2
ISBN 0-688-51811-7 lib. bdg.

Printed in the United States of America.
First Edition
1 2 3 4 5 6 7 8 9 10

For Mommy and Daddy
and my new niece
or nephew

An egg is to sit on

if you are a chicken.

A nose is to wash your back with

if you are an elephant.

Pockets are for your mother to keep
her children in

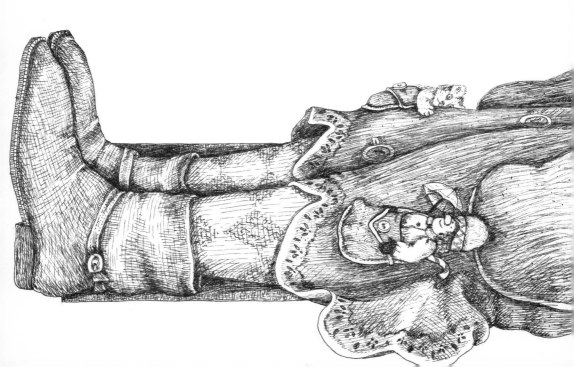

if you are a kangaroo.

A house is to eat for lunch

if you are a termite.

A ponytail is to swat flies with

if you are a pony.

Wings are what you'll get
when you grow up

if you are a caterpillar.

Legs are to make music with

if you are a grasshopper.

About the Author and Artist

CHRISTINE TANZ holds a B.A. from Radcliffe College and a Ph.D. from the University of Chicago. She currently teaches psychology at the University of Arizona, in Tucson, where she lives. Her special interest in the development of thinking and language in children helped hatch the idea for *An Egg Is to Sit On*, her first children's book.

ROSEKRANS HOFFMAN is a painter whose work has been exhibited in a number of galleries and museums. *An Egg Is to Sit On* is the fifth children's book she has illustrated; the first, *Walter in Love* by Alicen White, was also published by Lothrop.